SMALL PRAYERS

GREG MITCHELL

LION
Giftlines

Rita Murphy
A lovely woman
with lots of love

Copyright © 1995 Greg Mitchell

The author asserts the moral right
to be identified as the author of this work

First published in Australia in 1995 by
Dove, an imprint of HarperCollins*Publishers* (Australia) Pty Ltd
First published in the UK in 1997 by
Lion Publishing plc
Sandy Lane West, Oxford, England
ISBN 0 7459 3820 5

First edition 1997
10 9 8 7 6 5 4 3 2 1 0

A catalogue record for this book is available from the British Library

Designed by William Hung
Cover design by William Hung
Cover illustration by Kim Roberts, based on an illustration concept by Greg Mitchell
Illustrations by Greg Mitchell
Printed and bound in Malta by Interprint

ON THE MEANING OF LIFE AND A FEW MORE IMPORTANT QUESTIONS

Sometimes life is extremely busy.

Dear God, Why do all the best things happen when I'm too busy to enjoy them? Amen.

Or perhaps it's just that life keeps interrupting my imagination . . .

Dear God, Am I a figment of your imagination or the other way around? Amen.

When I do get the chance to sit down and think about it God often sneaks up and overpowers me . . .

Dear God, If what you see is what you get there must be an awful lot of you! Amen.

But sometimes it is not the big but the really small that gets me thinking.

Dear God, Do fleas ever have smaller fleas of their own? Amen.

However, it all comes down to a relationship between God and me . . .

Dear God, Do you enjoy my company or do all these questions get you down? Amen.

But in the end I'd hate to think that God treats me as badly as I treat him . . .

Dear God, I know you're really busy but could you spare a minute . . .

<u>DEAR</u> GOD

Just how much

do I have to suffer

from the little children?

Amen

DEAR GOD

Do you ever say

"Oops!"?

Amen

DEAR GOD

Make my heart beat quicker
than my fists.

Amen

DEAR GOD

In the great jigsaw of life

where do my bits fit?

Amen

DEAR GOD

Why did you choose my hands

to demonstrate

the right not knowing

what the left is doing?

Amen

DEAR GOD

Remind me
that turtles believe
that they are fast.

Amen

DEAR GOD

How many of my relations

are in my relationships?

Amen

DEAR GOD

Give me

the kinds of riches

that do not involve

threading camels.

Amen

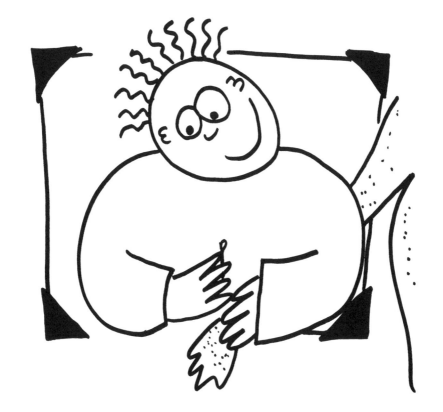

DEAR GOD

How come

I can't tolerate

intolerant people?

Amen

DEAR GOD

Help me to remember

that my conversations

with you

are not metered calls.

Amen

DEAR GOD

Does empowerment

always have to be

a shocking experience?

Amen

DEAR GOD

How did Mary and Joseph cope . . .

when Jesus was eighteen?

Amen

DEAR GOD

Help me

to grow

smaller.

Amen

DEAR GOD

Can you change

the scale

on my personal map?

Amen

DEAR GOD

Teach me
that feeling has more
to do with the heart
than the skin.

Amen

DEAR GOD

Why is it

that I can love other people . . .

until I start driving a car?

Amen

DEAR GOD

How long must I wait
until I stop being
impatient?

Amen

<u>DEAR</u> GOD

Could you send me

a postcard

when I'm too busy

on the phone?

Amen

DEAR GOD

How come you get the credit

when I'm good

and I get the blame

when I'm bad?

Amen

DEAR GOD

Help me to jump

over my errors

and not to trip

and fall on them.

Amen

DEAR GOD

If I don't behave myself

will you stop the car

and make me walk home?

Amen

DEAR GOD

Make me more confident

of my own opinions . . .

if that's all right with you.

Amen

DEAR GOD

Will I ever reach

perfexshun?

Amen

<u>DEAR</u> GOD

Remind me that while I like to know
what is good about me,
others need to know
what is great about them.

Amen

DEAR GOD

Can I punch out anyone

who does not believe

in peace and love?

Amen

DEAR GOD

Help me to long for

the knowledge

that will shorten

my ignorance.

Amen

DEAR GOD

How well

do you listen?

Amen

DEAR GOD

Teach me

that the heaviest load

to carry

is a grudge.

Amen

DEAR GOD

What else

is there?

Amen

DEAR GOD

Remind me
that winners
do not always
come first.

Amen

DEAR GOD

As far as commandments go . . .

is five out of ten

still a pass?

Amen

DEAR GOD

Help me to remember

that you made me

AND

everyone else as well.

Amen

DEAR GOD

Allow me to feel

safe enough

to live dangerously.

Amen

DEAR GOD

Were the loaves and fishes

a miracle . . .

or was Jesus just a great cook?

Amen

DEAR GOD

Provide me

with the combination

of loving events

that will open my safe heart.

Amen

DEAR GOD

Do you

believe in

atheists?

Amen

DEAR GOD

Help me to live

here and now,

not there or was,

or then and maybe.

Amen

DEAR GOD

When my head
begins to swell
send me a safety helmet
two sizes too small.

Amen

D E A R GOD

Teach others

that nothing distracts

my depression more

than a live present.

Amen

<u>DEAR</u> GOD

How many stages

must I go through

before there are no stages left?

Amen

DEAR GOD

What would Jesus say

to the media?

Amen

DEAR GOD

Help me

not to confuse

people's volume

with their capacity.

Amen

DEAR GOD

If I plant

the mustard seed of the kingdom

in my heart

will there be enough room for it to grow?

Amen

DEAR GOD

Can I fight the good fight

without physical pain?

Amen

DEAR GOD

Why do I ask

so many questions?

Amen

DEAR GOD

Teach me to smell

when my hopes

are too high.

Amen

DEAR GOD

Just how much

do you know?

Amen

DEAR GOD

Do not let

the octopus of preoccupation

squeeze the life

out of today.

Amen

DEAR GOD

Could the blots

in my copybook

be works of art?

Amen

DEAR GOD

Teach me

that every day

is a New Year's Day.

Amen

DEAR GOD

Do you listen to prayers
that are really angry
with you?

Amen

DEAR GOD

Take my ego

and make it flatter.

Amen

DEAR GOD

Thank you

for all of creation.

The sun

must have been fun.

Amen

DEAR GOD

If you are found
in the quiet places,
how come children
seem to find you so easily?

Amen

DEAR GOD

Is waking up

each day

like a miniature

resurrection?

Amen

DEAR GOD

Have mercy

on me

a thinner.

Amen

DEAR GOD

How come

some people seem to know

exactly what

you are thinking?

Amen

DEAR GOD

In your magnificence,
in all your beauty and strength,
in everything that comes from you,
and which is owed to you . . .
thank you for short prayers.

Amen